First Lessons® Dulcimer
DAD Tuning
by Joyce Ochs

Online Audio

www.melbay.com/98388BCDEB

T0104238

CONTENTS

Acknowledgment: I would like to acknowledge and thank John McClure, owner and sound technician of Jonymac Studio, Louisville, KY, for the professional advice, guitar accompaniments and expert musicianship he provided for me in producing this *First Lessons audio recording*. Every "first-time" recording experience would be greatly enhanced by his guidance and encouragement!

Welcome to the Lap Dulcimer!

You have purchased a music book that will enable you to begin learning to play a beautiful American folk instrument that will provide many hours of enjoyment and fun for you and your family and friends. Remember that this instrument is truly a folk instrument—one that was often played by untrained musicians who were taught by their aunts or grandpas or neighbors. It is known as a very "friendly" instrument and can be mastered by many who feel that their musical abilities are limited. If you have the *desire* to learn to play your lap dulcimer, you can!

◆ Elements of Music

Music has three main components: melody, rhythm, and accompaniment or chord structure. The **melody** is the tune or the "ups and downs" of the pitches and notes. **Rhythm** is the duration of each of those notes. In order for

a song to be recognizable it must have a melody and a rhythm pattern. Songs also have an **accompaniment** or chord structure or which adds a lot of interest and feeling to the tune. You will be learning how to read melody, rhythm and chord structures in this book. There are many other ways to enhance and embellish music through dynamics, phrasing and expression which allow the performer to personalize the music he or she plays.

◆ Holding Your Dulcimer

The traditional way to hold the lap dulcimer is as shown. Even if you are left-handed (and I am!) I suggest that you place the head/tuning pegs toward the left of your body. We use both hands to play the dulcimer and I find it much easier to play my instrument in this position rather than reversing the strings, placing the head of my dulcimer to my right side, and altering many instructions. Your feet need to be flat on the floor, knees spread far enough apart so your dulcimer can balance and sit evenly on your thighs. And ladies . . . a long skirt or pants are necessary!

◆ Illustration/Parts of the Lap Dulcimer

Study the illustration below and become familiar with the parts of the lap dulcimer. You will be using this illustration in the lessons which follow this introductory section.

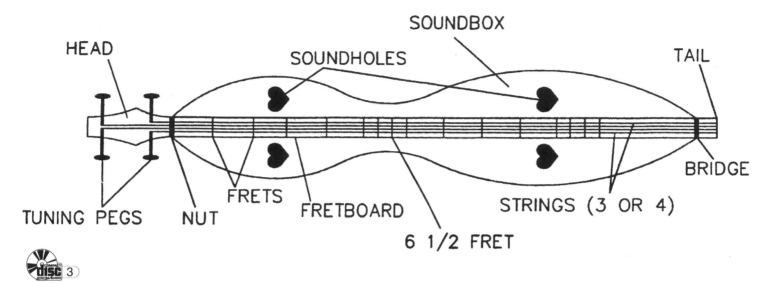

◆ Tuning Your Dulcimer to DAD

To tune means to adjust to the proper pitch. When you tune your dulcimer, you will adjust each string to match a pre-determined pitch. Dulcimers can be tuned to a variety of pitches to form different modes. *As indicated on the cover of this instruction book, you will be tuning to DAD, which is an increasingly popular tuning for the lap dulcimer.* DAD is a very versatile tuning, provides a major scale with the 6 1/2 fret and chords can be made flexible by inverting the bass and melody fretting. More on that later.

If you've never tuned a string instrument, don't panic! Even though this will seem quite a challenge the first few times, it will get easier! Hang in there! The accompanying recording will serve as an auditory aid in the process of tuning. Refer to the illustration below to identify your string names: **Bass** (the heavy string furthermost from your body), **Middle**, and **Melody** (closest to your body and may be double strung).

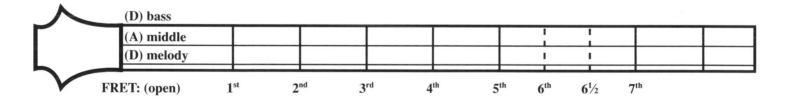

As indicated, we will be tuning the **Bass string to D** below middle C on a piano, the **Middle string to A** below middle C on a piano, and **the Melody string(s) to D** just above middle C on a piano. Experiment with the bass string tuning peg by turning it in both directions. Pluck the bass string and notice that the pitch gets higher or lower as you turn the tuning peg. Referring to the online audio (or a piano, electric tuner, pitch pipe, or other instrument) listen very carefully several times to the sound of the D pitch. Think about it in your head and perhaps hum it. Turn the bass tuning peg until the string pitch matches the D pitch. As you turn it, if the string pitch is getting further away from the desired D pitch, turn the tuning peg the other direction to move closer to the desired pitch. When you feel you hear a matched pitch, continue to turn the peg very slightly in each direction to see if you can tune even more closely to the desired pitch. Continue this process until you feel your bass string is exactly the same pitch as your source pitch.

Tune the middle string with the same process. This A string is a different pitch from the bass and melody strings. For now, use the online audio or other tuning source to tune this A. When you become used to tuning your instrument, you can fret your bass string on the 4th fret and match the middle string to that pitch (it's an A!). Now tune the melody string(s) to D above middle C. This pitch is exactly one octave higher than the bass string. Match the pitch exactly to your source pitch.

When you have tuned all of your strings, strum across all of them together to see if they sound in harmony with one another. Check them with the accompanying audio to make sure they match. If they don't, go back and retune from the beginning of this section on tuning. Don't give up! If you just can't seem to have success, find a friend or music shop to help you learn this process.

◆ **The 6 1/2 Fret**

Refer again to the illustration of the dulcimer and notice the location of the 6 1/2 fret. Your dulcimer may or may not have this fret and it will be helpful to know if it does. The easiest way to determine whether or not your instrument has this fret is to ask the person from whom you purchased it. If you are having your dulcimer made, request a 6 1/2 fret. If you are unable to determine this by asking someone, place your dulcimer across your lap as illustrated with the head and tuning pegs to your left. Look straight down at the middle of your fretboard, half way between the left and right ends. If you see four frets that are placed slightly closer together than the ones to the left of them, you probably have a 6 1/2 fret. This is good! When playing in DAD, the 6 1/2 fret is very useful and if you don't have one you will probably want it added later. A reputable dulcimer maker or string instrument repair shop can add this fret for you. Why? The 6 1/2 fret creates a major scale for you as you move your finger(s) up the melody string and you will want this pitch for many of your songs. However, you can get started playing right now without it! You will learn how to create a scale in Lesson One.

◆ **Basic Techniques**
   • **To Fret:** to press down on one or more strings just to the left of a specific fret in order to produce a desired pitch. (a left-hand activity)
   • **To Strum:** to stroke or drag across all of the strings with a pick or your fingers using a wrist action; you may strum away from or towards your body or in both directions. (A right-hand activity)
   • **To Open Strum:** to strum (with your right hand) without fretting (with your left hand). This will create a D Chord or D A D—the pitches we tuned your dulcimer to!
   • **To Pick/Pluck:** to set in motion or cause to vibrate (and therefore create a sound) a specific string by striking it with a pick or finger (a right-hand activity).
   • **To Slide:** to move from one fret to another without taking the finger entirely off the string (a left-hand activity).

With the information provided in this introduction, we are now ready to look at Lesson One and start to make music with our dulcimers. Always feel free to refer back to these beginning pages for reminders and clarification of definitions and illustrations. All musical terms and definitions are in **bold** print for quick location.

Lesson One

In Lesson One we are going to start at the very beginning by learning the melody and rhythm of several familiar tunes. By the end of this lesson you will be able to play these tunes on your dulcimer and hopefully sing along! In order to do this we need to become familiar with **dulcimer tablature,** which is the written instructions and information that enable a person to produce the music which is on the written page.

◆ **Reading Dulcimer Tablature**

The tablature for notating the lap dulcimer is made up of a standard **treble clef staff** (five closely spaced lines connected with a treble clef sign) and three lines below, spaced further apart which represent the strings on your lap dulcimer. **Bar lines** divide the staff into **measures** or units of rhythm.

| | measure | bar line | measure | bar line | measure | bar line |

Treble Staff

Dulcimer Strings
D
A
D

You are aware that musical scores have a variety of notes that give information about the melody and rhythm of the music. In addition to these notes on the treble staff we will be looking at numbers on the lower three lines which will instruct us how to produce melodies on our dulcimer.

◆ **Strumming Note Values (right hand activity)**

First let's work with rhythm. Practicing the notes values and **strumming the dulcimer is a right hand activity**. Hold a **pick** (a small triangular piece of plastic or nylon) with your right-hand thumb and index finger. With one point of the pick facing down, stroke across all of the strings creating a tone with each string. Strum away from your body.

On the following page you see **standard rhythmic notation** for four musical note values. Each of the patterns represents four steady beats—like a clock pendulum or a heart beat. A **beat** is one unit of time, as in the "tick-tick-tick-tick" of a clock (four beats). Study and practice each illustration and strum as indicated. The **repeat sign** (two dots followed by a double line) tells you to repeat the sequence.

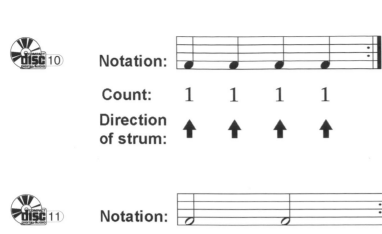

Notation: **Count:** 1 1 1 1 **Direction of strum:** ↑ ↑ ↑ ↑

QUARTER NOTE: Strum once for each note you see. Keep the strums steady like the "tick tick" of a clock. Strum away from your body.

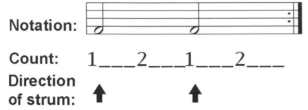

Notation: **Count:** 1___2___1___2___ **Direction of strum:** ↑   ↑

HALF NOTE: Strum once as you say "one"; let the sound continue as you say "two". Strum away from your body. Repeat the sequence.

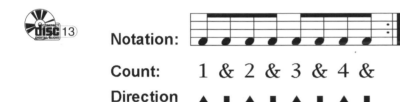

Notation: **Count:** 1___2___3___4___ **Direction of strum:** ↑

WHOLE NOTE: Strum on one; let the sound continue through beats 2-3-4. Strum away from your body Repeat the sequence.

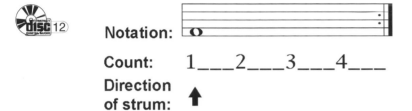

Notation: **Count:** 1 & 2 & 3 & 4 & **Direction of strum:** ↑ ↓ ↑ ↓ ↑ ↓ ↑ ↓

EIGHTH NOTES: Strum away from your body on the beats (1-2-3-4) and toward your body on the "ands" (&). This is a divided beat; all strumming (away and toward the body) has the same rhythmic value (tick-tick-tick-tick). These are fast notes. There are 2 eighth notes to each quarter note.

Each of the note values above has a corresponding **rest** or period of silence instead of sound. When a rest appears in the music you are silent for the beat value. Below is an illustration of the rests which correspond to the note values you've learned above.

NOTE AND REST EQUIVALENTS

| QUARTER | | HALF | | WHOLE | | EIGHTH | |
| NOTE | REST | NOTE | REST | NOTE | REST | NOTE | REST |

◆ Melody and the D Major Scale (left hand activity)

Now we need to learn how to locate melody tones for our songs. The placement of the notes on the treble clef determines how low or high the tones are. Notice that the **D Major scale** is a series of 8 consecutive tones/notes which move from low to high on the treble staff. The pitches you hear when you play the scale will also move from low to high. The 1st and the 8th pitches will both be D's, one octave (or eight notes) apart.

D Major Scale

Note Name	D	E	F#	G	A	B	C#	D
Fret # on dulcimer	0	1	2	3	4	5	6 1/2	7

Now study the illustration below of the dulcimer fretboard. Let's create a musical scale by moving our left hand index finger along the melody strings(s) just to the left of each fret while **plucking** (vibrating a single string or melody strings) with your right hand. For now we won't strum across all the strings. This will allow you to hear the melody scale more clearly.

	(D) bass								
	(A) middle								
	(D) melody	E	F#	G	A	B	C		D
FRET:	(open)	1st	2nd	3rd	4th	5th	6th		7th

	(D) bass									
	(A) middle									
	(D) melody	E	F#	G	A	B	C	C#	D	
FRET:	(open)	1st	2nd	3rd	4th	5th	6th	6½	7th	

Pluck the "open" melody string. **"Open"** means no fret is being pressed. This is D, the pitch you tuned to when we tuned your instrument. Now press your left index finger just to the left of the first fret on the melody string. Pluck the same string with your right hand; it should sound one pitch higher (E) on the scale than open D. Continue moving to the right across the fretboard pressing just to the left of each fret with your left index finger while plucking the string(s) with your right hand. (Remember to skip the 6th fret and play the 6 1/2 instead.) Stop after you have played the 7th fret. That pitch should be one octave higher than the open D you played first. Hopefully you heard an ascending scale as you moved toward the right of your fretboard . . . did you? If not, reread this paragraph and try it again! Note: if you don't have a 6 1/2 fret, you will hear a lowered tone when you play the 6th fret. If your tones sound muffled or "tinny", there are two things to check. First, make sure that you are *pressing down just hard enough* on the string to create a clear tone and secondly, make sure you are pressing down *just to the left* of the fret needed. Those two things should produce nice clear tones on your dulcimer.

You have now learned some skills for creating rhythm and melody on your dulcimer. So, we should be able to work on some familiar tunes! For now, we are only going to be working with the melody string line. We will **drone** (strum the strings open without changing pitch) the middle and bass strings.

Boil Them Cabbage is a perfect tune to start every new dulcimer student with even if they don't know the tune! Why? Because the rhythm is all quarter notes and the melody is very repetitive! Does that sound easy? It is! Let's look at the tablature. Remember that the bottom three lines represent the strings of your dulcimer. Look at the **melody** line. Notice the 2 2 2 2 / 3 3 3 3 /2 2 2 2 /1 1 1 1—these numbers tell you which frets to press down on with your left hand (remember the scale exercise) while strumming with your right hand. Try playing this song. Repeat it until it feels comfortable and you can play it with a steady rhythm.

BOIL THEM CABBAGE

MELODY ONLY

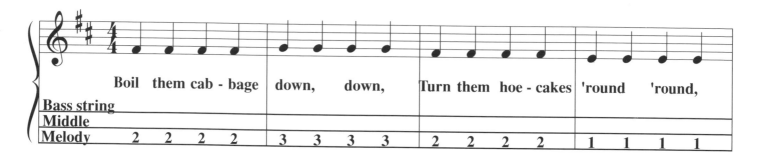

Notice the numeric fraction 4/4 in the treble clef at the beginning of the song above. This **time signature** helps us organize the rhythmic feel of our music. The top number tells us that there are 4 beats (tick-tick-tick tick) in each measure. The bottom number tells us what kind of note value gets one beat—in this case the quarter note.

Here are two more songs to practice on using the melody string tablature. They have the same time signature so there are 4 beats in each measure.

HOT CROSS BUNS
MELODY ONLY

Did you notice the quarter notes, half notes and eighth notes? You probably know this song and the familiarity of it will reinforce correct note values. If you don't know it, clap the rhythm pattern several times before you try playing the melody line on your dulcimer.

This next song is a traditional Appalachian folk tune. If you don't know it you may want to clap or open strum (right-hand activity) the rhythm pattern several times before adding the melody line (left-hand activity).

GO TELL AUNT RHODY
MELODY ONLY

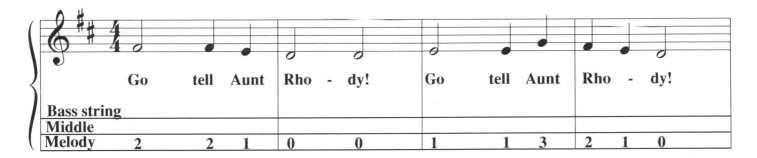

Go		tell	Aunt	Rho	-	dy!	Go		tell	Aunt	Rho	-	dy!

Bass string

Middle

Melody — 2 — 2 — 1 — 0 — 0 — 1 — 1 — 3 — 2 — 1 — 0

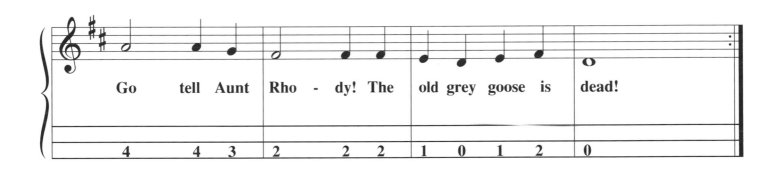

Go		tell	Aunt	Rho	-	dy! The	old grey goose is	dead!

4 — 4 — 3 — 2 — 2 — 2 — 1 — 0 — 1 — 2 — 0

Lesson Two

In Lesson Two we are going to embellish the melodies we learned in Lesson One by adding an accompaniment. In order to do this we need to learn three chords that will make our melodies sound like songs! A **chord** is a combination of two or more tones that help to create a tonal base or "home base" for the tune.

◆ Three Very Friendly Chords!

Although there are many, many chords to choose from you will find these three the most useful for your first songs. They are the foundation chords for all the music you will be playing. Practice them until they are good friends; memorize their fret numbers. They are the most important chords in the key of D.

♩ Basic D Chord

Prepare yourself for some good news! The basic D chord is "open"— there is no fretting with your left hand! Remember how we tuned your dulcimer to DAD? Those pitches create a basic D chord. Note that the tablature in the right illustration below reads **0-0-0**. (These numbers are vertical on the tablature line of your music.) These numbers tell you which frets to press with your left hand — in this case you don't press any frets. You have been playing this chord all along as you practiced your right hand strumming!

♩ Basic A Chord

In order to create the pitches we need for the A chord we have to press on certain frets to alter the pitches of the strings. Notice the **1-0-1** tablature in the right illustration below. These numbers tell us which frets to press for each string. The "X"'s on the fretboard illustration tell us to press just to the left of the fret indicated by the number on each string. For the A chord we will need to press just to the left of the 1st fret on the bass string and just to the left of the 1st fret of the melody string. The middle string remains open — **(0)**. Practice four beats of this A Chord and then four beats of the basic D Chord above. Practice this sequence until you can move comfortably back and forth from the two chords. A suggested fingering for this A chord is your 2nd finger (left hand) on the bass string and your 4th finger (left hand) on the melody string.

♩ Basic G Chord

The G chord uses a different combination of fretting since we need different pitches. Look at the illustrations below. You see a **0-1-3** on the right one. As indicated, we need to fret the middle string 1st fret and the melody string 3rd fret. Notice that the bass string is open — **(0)**. Practice four beats of this G Chord followed by four beats of the basic D Chord. Practice this sequence until you can move back and forth from one chord to the other. A suggested fingering for this G chord is your 3rd finger on the middle string 1st fret and your thumb on the melody string 3rd fret.

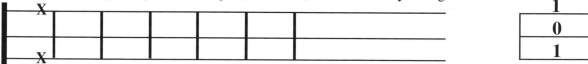

These chords will be extremely useful for the music that follows in this book. Many songs can be played with these three chords as an accompaniment. Practice them as quarter notes until they feel very comfortable and you can move from one to another without pausing or stopping.

◆ Embellishing Tunes with Chords

We will start by adding chords to the songs we learned in Lesson One. The melody line (bottom line of the tablature) will remain the same. We will be adding chord tablature on the other two strings. Now, here is an important rule that you might want to read several times before continuing with these songs.

The melody tablature <u>always overrides</u> the basic chord tablature.

This means that your melody remains as it is written and is more important than the chord. Always play your melody fret even if it doesn't coincide with the chord that accompanies it. (If you don't, you will loose the tune of the song!)

Notice, also, that the chord names are printed above the staff of every song; you may refer to these to help identify the chords.

The melody line for **Boil Them Cabbage** is exactly the same as in Lesson One. You now see that the D, A and G chords have been added to the bass and middle strings. Try playing this song adding the chords along with the melody. Play line one until it feels comfortable and you can play with a steady beat. Then try line two; it is very similar to the first line.

BOIL THEM CABBAGE

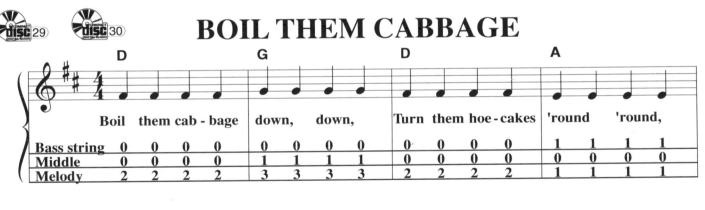

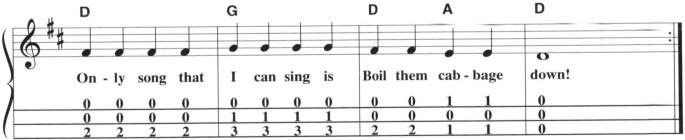

Let's try another Lesson One tune, **Hot Cross Buns**. You'll be alternating the D and A chords with each quarter note. Remember to use more than one left-hand finger on the melody string. The thumb is very useful when reaching for melody frets toward the right.

HOT CROSS BUNS

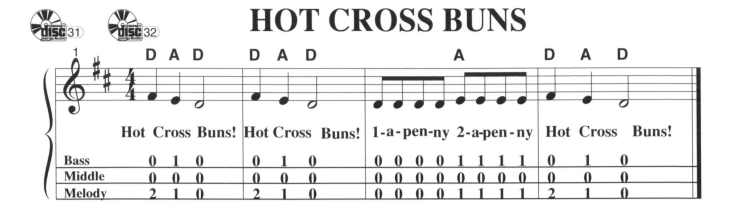

How did it go? Are you ready to try **Go Tell Aunt Rhody** with chords? You are probably realizing how important it is to use more than just your index finger on the melody string. For example, when you play the A chord in measure three, use your thumb to reach the 3rd fret on the word "Aunt". Slide your thumb down to the 2nd fret on the syllable "Rho". Then you'll find yourself back to the A chord (1-0-1). Notice in measure seven that you need to lift your finger off the melody string on the word "grey" in order to hear the correct melody tone. Let's try it!

GO TELL AUNT RHODY

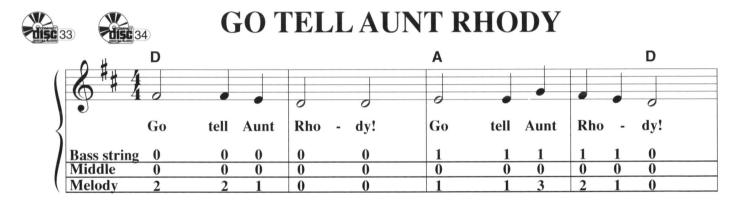

◆ **Adding New Songs to Our Repertoire**

Here are some additional familiar tunes to work on. They will provide practice working on melody and chords. Play the songs slowly until they sound rhythmically correct. Remember to use more than one left-hand finger when fretting the melody. Your music will sound smoother and you can keep a steadier beat. Have fun!

MERRILY WE ROLL ALONG
(MARY HAD A LITTLE LAMB)

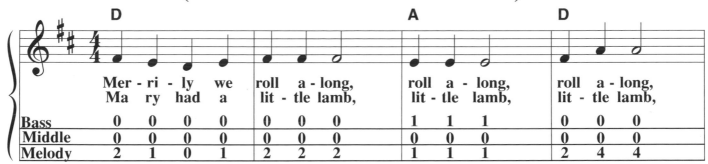

	Mer - ri - ly we			roll a - long,			roll a - long,			roll a - long,	
	Ma - ry had a			lit - tle lamb,			lit - tle lamb,			lit - tle lamb,	
Bass	0	0	0	0	0	0	1	1	1	0	0	0
Middle	0	0	0	0	0	0	0	0	0	0	0	0
Melody	2	1	0	1	2	2	2	1	1	1	2	4	4

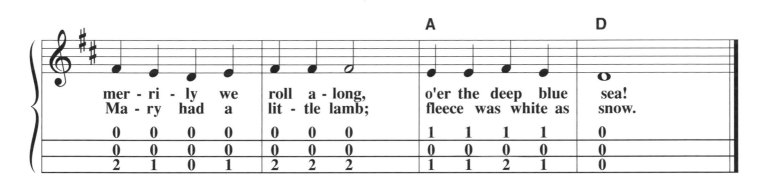

mer - ri - ly we			roll a - long,			o'er the deep blue			sea!
Ma - ry had a			lit - tle lamb;			fleece was white as			snow.
0	0	0	0	0	0	1	1	1	0
0	0	0	0	0	0	0	0	0	0
2	1	0	1	2	2	2	1	1	2	1	0

LONDON BRIDGE

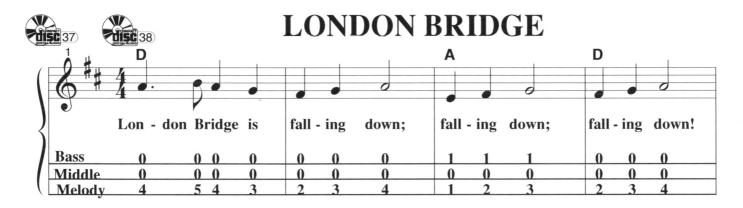

	Lon - don Bridge is			fall - ing down;			fall - ing down;			fall - ing down!	
Bass	0	0	0	0	0	0	1	1	1	0	0	0
Middle	0	0	0	0	0	0	0	0	0	0	0	0
Melody	4	5	4	3	2	3	4	1	2	3	2	3	4

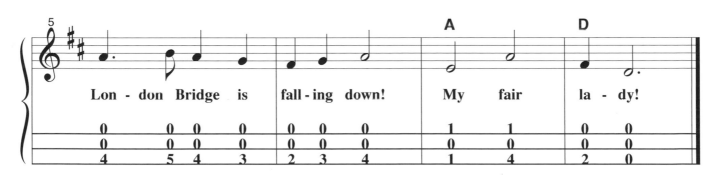

Lon - don Bridge is			fall - ing down!			My fair		la - dy!
0	0	0	0	0	0	1	1	0	0
0	0	0	0	0	0	0	0	0	0
4	5	4	3	2	3	4	1	4	2	0

Notice the dots after the quarter notes in measures one and five. They are followed by eighth notes. This creates an uneven rhythm pattern—like the gallop of a horse or a child skipping. You will probably play the rhythm correctly as you sing along!

Lesson Three

So far, all of the tunes we've learned have started on or above **D**, the first tone of the musical scale. Therefore we have always played the melody exclusively on the melody string.

◆ Dipping Down to the Middle String

Many songs start below D or below the open melody string on your dulcimer. How can we play a tone lower than open D on your melody string? We can't! But, the middle string is tuned lower than the melody string D, isn't it? Remember we tuned it to **A** below the melody string D. This middle string will allow us to play pitches below the melody string. Look at the exercise below.

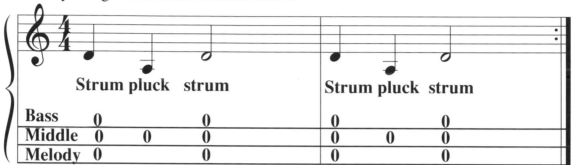

As you know, the **0-0-0** indicates a strum of the D chord. The **0** which follows instructs you to pluck or pick the middle string (notice that the **0** sits on the middle string) without strumming the other two strings. In other words you will only hear the middle string **A**. Then you are instructed to strum the D chord again. Practice this exercise several times until you can play it rhythmically correct. Do you recognize the last phrase of **Frere Jacque**? (Din Dan Dong! Din Dan Dong!)

Now let's look at the whole tune, **Frere Jacque**. The first line is very simple; try it several times. Measures 5 and 6 have a series of eighth notes; they're going to be faster aren't they? Plan your melody string fingering so you can keep your eighth notes steady. You can either slide your thumb or index finger up and down the frets or you can use different fingers for each fret — whichever is more efficient for you.

FRERE JACQUE
(Dip to the middle string)

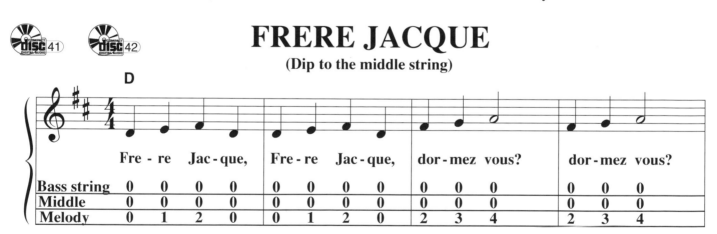

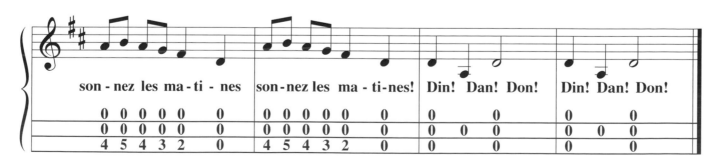

Remember that any time you see a single number on your tablature it means to pluck that string rather than strum across all of the strings. Here are some more tunes that require you to dip down onto the middle string to find your melody pitches. Sometimes you have to fret the middle string to locate the correct pitch. The tablature will indicate your fret with a number just as it does on your melody string.

SKIP TO MY LOU

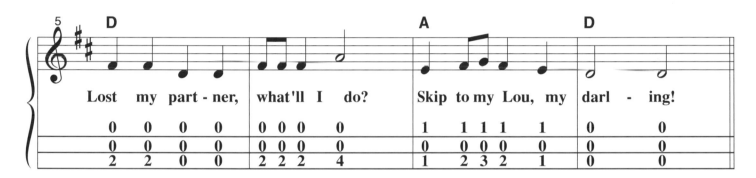

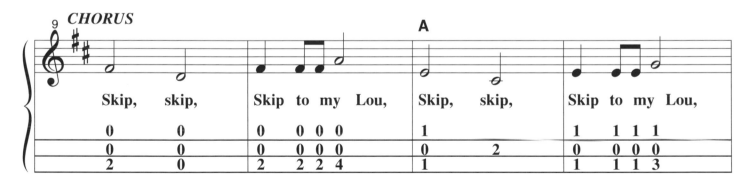

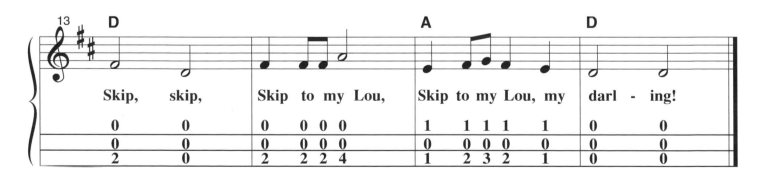

There are several new musical ideas which occur in this song. You will notice that the 1st three notes in each line are plucked. Do not strum across all of your strings. This is to produce a nice clear melody. Now look at the last two measures of each line. You will notice dotted half notes. Each of these dotted half notes get 3 beats. You will also see a curved line connecting these notes. This curved line is called a tie. A **tie** connects the value of the two notes together. We will play the 1st note and hold the tone through the value of the 2nd note (6 beats in this case).

DOWN IN THE VALLEY

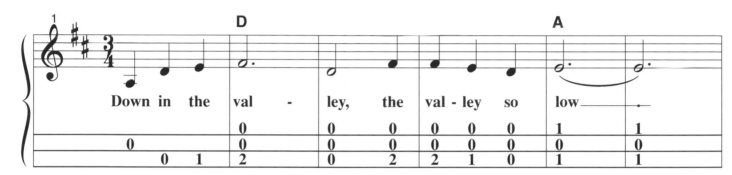

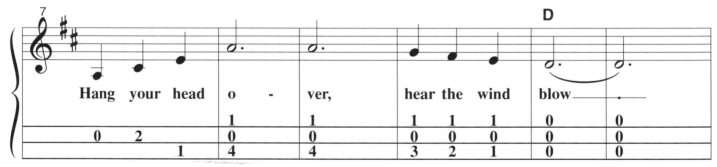

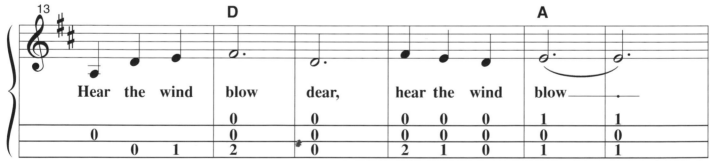

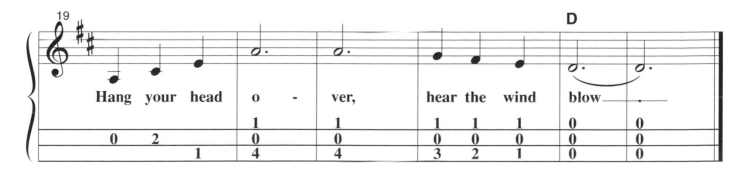

◆ Adding the "Dum-diddy"!

As you become more comfortable and proficient with your dulcimer playing, you may find that you would like to embellish your tunes and provide some rhythmic interest. One of the easiest ways to accomplish this is by substituting a simple rhythmic pattern for half notes in your musical scores. Say "dum-diddy" four times in a row. Now repeat the sequence again and clap the rhythm of the words as you say them. You have just mastered the dum-diddy rhythm pattern. Now let's see what it looks like on a musical score.

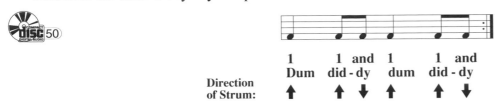

Practice this exercise until it becomes familiar. Be sure to observe the arrows which indicate the direction of your strumming (away from or towards your body).

Now return to **Hot Cross Buns** and **Go Tell Aunt Rhody** for a few minutes in Lesson One. Try playing each of these songs and *substitute* a dum-diddy for each half-note in the songs. Since one dum-diddy equals one half- note, you will be replacing the half-notes with the dum-diddy. This may take a while to get use to, but once you do, you will want to use dum-diddys in all of your songs. Just remember, dum-diddys can replace any half note value in any song. They sound very impressive!

Now for a few more fun songs to work on in this chapter!

THREE JOLLY FISHERMEN

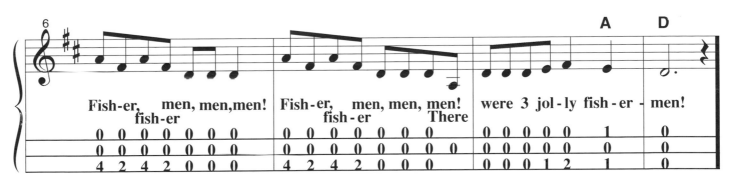

Vs. 2. The first one's name was Abraham
(Repeat)
Abra, Abra, ham, ham ham
(Repeat)
The first one's name was Abraham.

Vs. 3. The second one's name was Issac
I, I, sac, sac, sac.

Vs. 4. The third one's name was Jacob
Ja, Ja, cup, cup cup

Vs. 5. They all went down to Jericho
Jeri, Jeri, cho, cho, cho

Vs. 6. They wished they'd gone to Amsterdam
Amster, Amster, shhh, shhh, shhh!

In measures five and six you may want to anchor your left-hand 2nd finger on the 2nd fret and just press your thumb onto the 4th fret when the tablature calls for it.

POLLY WOLLY DOODLE

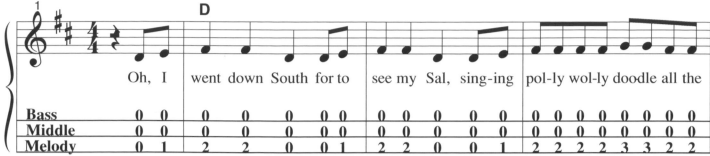

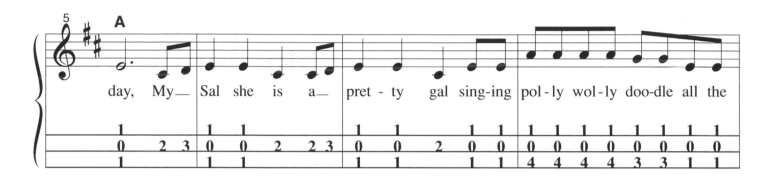

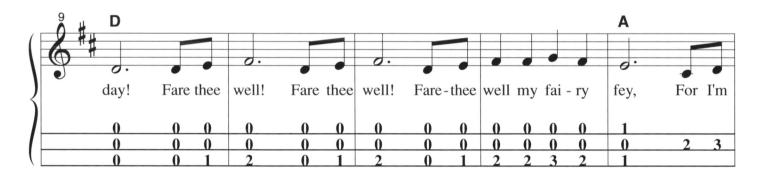

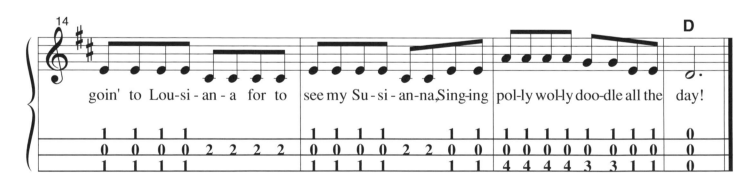

In measures 5, 6, 7, 13, 14, and 15, pluck the middle string as indicated.

Simple Gifts is a lovely shaker tune that is a favorite among dulcimer players. If you are not familiar with the melody, work very slowly — there are alot of eighth notes! Notice the G chords in measures 9 and 17 . They are called **inverted chords** because they are upside-down. Remember our original G chord (0-1-3); it now appears as 3-1-0. We can do this because both the bass string and the melody strings are tuned to D. In this case we inverted the chord because the melody requires a D. You will learn more about inverted chords in Lesson Five.

SIMPLE GIFTS
(Shaker Tune)

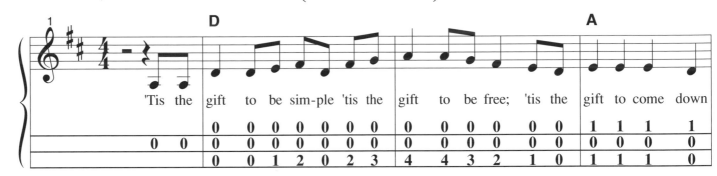

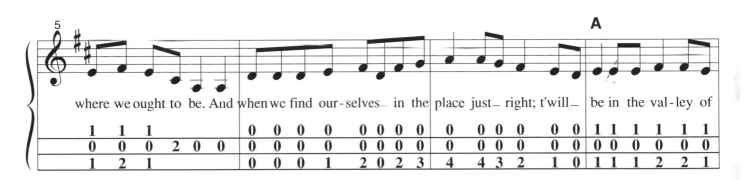

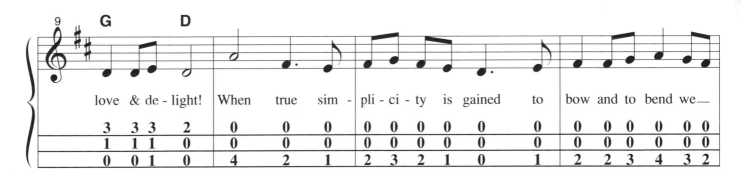

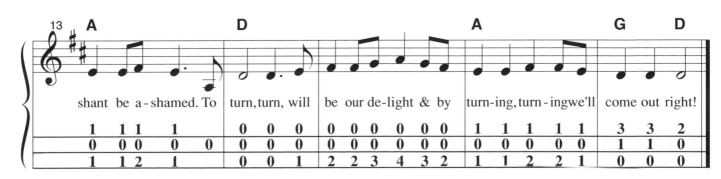

Lesson Four

In Lesson Three we concentrated on songs that dipped below D on your dulcimer. In this lesson we will move up the fretboard with higher melodies. This will enable us to expand our chord positions and options.

◆ A New Look and Slightly Different Sound

As you have now experienced, you can play a number of songs with the D, G, and A chords. We will now work on some melodies that require us to play the same chords in a higher position on the fretboard because of the melody line. We will also learn several more chords with will make our music sound even more elaborate!

♩ High G Chord

This chord has the same notes as the G chord you learned in Lesson Two. However, it is pitched higher to enable us to play higher melody notes in the following songs. The bass and middle strings are fretted on the 3rd fret and the melody string is fretted on the 5th fret. Find this chord on your dulcimer and practice moving back and forth from the earlier D chord to this one until it feels comfortable and you can keep a steady beat.

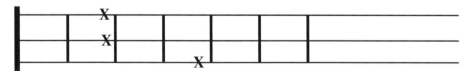

◆ Sliding Down the Fretboard

♩ F♯ minor Chord

This is a very pretty chord that I use often to slide down a melody sequence. Find it on your fretboard and notice that each of the pitches is one fret lower than the High G chord. The fret numbers are **2-2-4** while the G chord is **3-3-5**. Practice moving from the G chord to the F♯ minor chord by locking your left hand fingers in position for the G chord and then simply slide your left hand one fret position to the left. Move your whole hand; not each finger. Practice alternating 4 beats of the G chord followed by 4 beats of the F♯ minor chord until it feels comfortable.

♩ E minor Chord

I have some more good news! Look at the illustration of the E minor chord . . . notice a pattern? It's a **1-1-3**. Each pitch is 1 fret lower than the F♯ minor chord. Find it on your dulcimer and practice the sequence G chord, F♯ minor chord, and E minor chord using quarter notes for each chord. Remember to keep your left hand locked in the G chord position and just move to the left one fret for each new chord. You will be using this sequence in several of the songs that follow.

Here are some great songs using the chords and musical techniques described above. You are probably familiar with all these songs. This makes learning more friendly, doesn't it?

KUM BA YA!

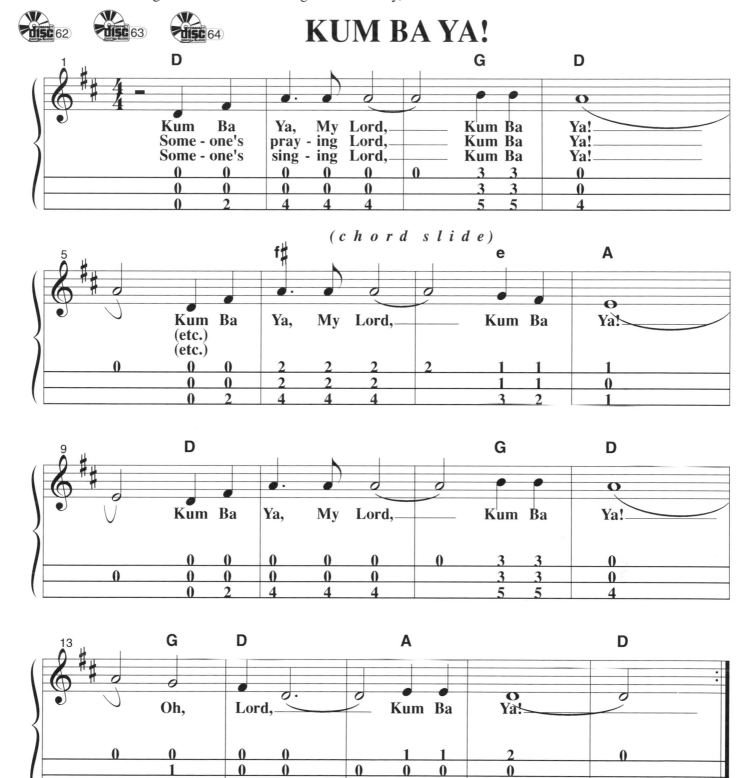

Notice that the bass and middle strings have some "plucked" notes to add musical interest during tied notes which are held quite long in this song.

THIS OLD MAN

(chord slide)

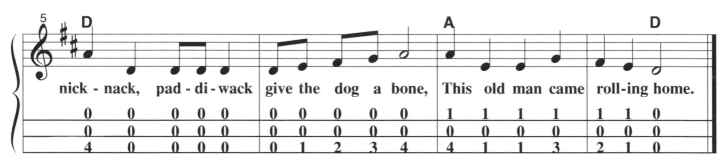

On the *chord slide* (measure # 3) remember to lock your left hand in position for the G chord and simply move down the fretboard for each new chord (f#, e, and D).

MICHAEL, ROW THE BOAT ASHORE

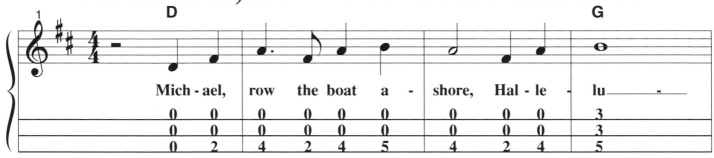

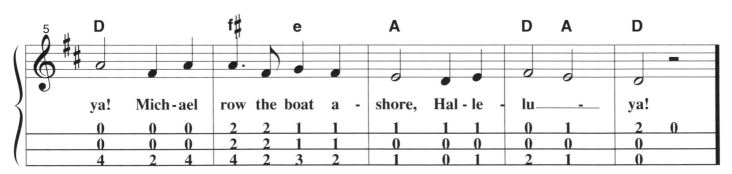

Notice the "2-0" on the bass string in the very last measure; it's just another decorative ending to the song to make it sound finished!

OH! SUSANNA

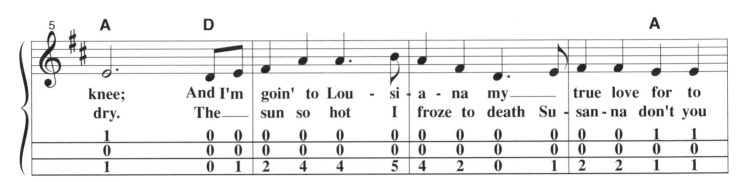

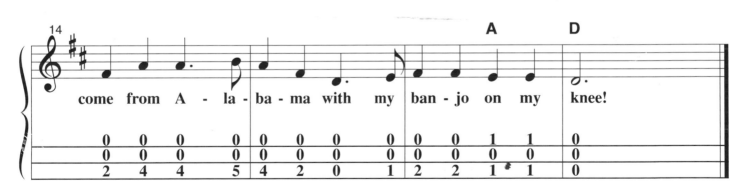

The **repeat sign** (two dots followed by a double bar line) just preceding the chorus instructs you to go back to the beginning and sing the 2nd line of text before singing the chorus.

WHEN THE SAINTS GO MARCHING IN!

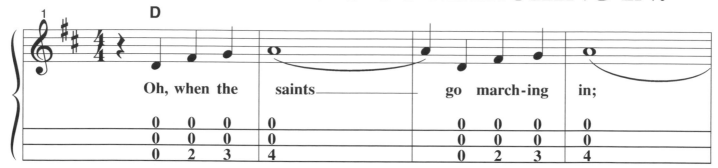

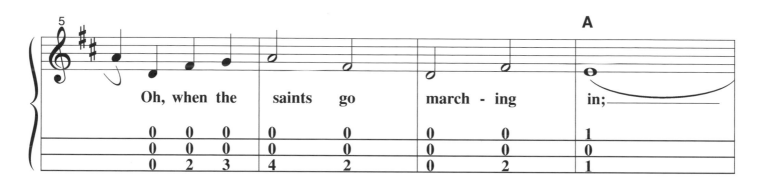

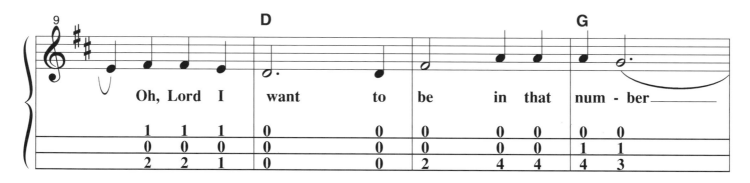

This song gives you another chance to use the "dum-diddy" pattern during the tied notes. You can play two dum-diddys for each whole note followed by one extra "dum" for the tied quarter note.

LITTLE LIZA JANE

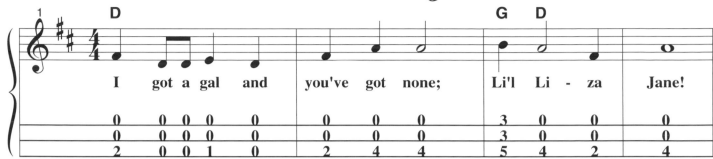

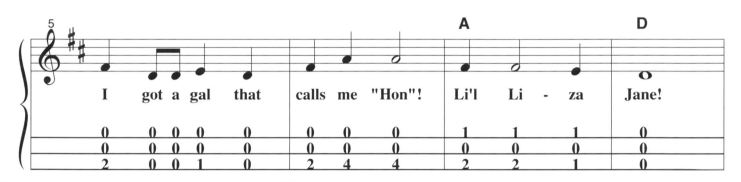

Notice the slides in measures 9-12 and 13-14; lock your left hand in the 0-5-4 position in measure 9 and simply slide your fingers up or down the frets as indicated. Your bass string is open!

Lesson Five

By adding several more chords to your repertoire your song possibilities will become almost endless in the DAD tuning. You will find these chords in all DAD dulcimer books that you purchase. If you play by ear you will also find that these chords will become useful as you experiment with new music.

◆ A Few More Chords!

These three chords do not need very much explanation; you know how to locate each fret of the chord. Practice each new chord by strumming it four times followed by four strums of the basic D chord. Repeat the sequence several times. You wil find these chords in the songs that follow in this chapter. Remember that the chords are always labelled just above the musical score of each linein the songs.

♩ A^7 Chord

♩ E Chord (E Major/E^7/E minor)

This versatile chord can serve as three different E chords because of the tones it creates. Any time your tablature calls for an E chord you are safe with this one!

♩ B minor Chord

Notice that the B minor chord has a **0** for the melody string fret; we need the open D for this chord.

Let's try some new songs using the chords above!

OLD JOE CLARK

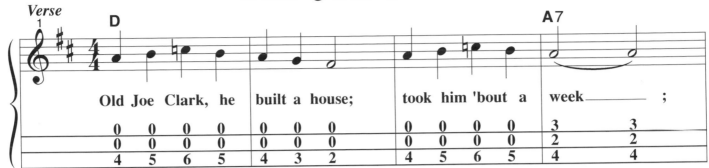

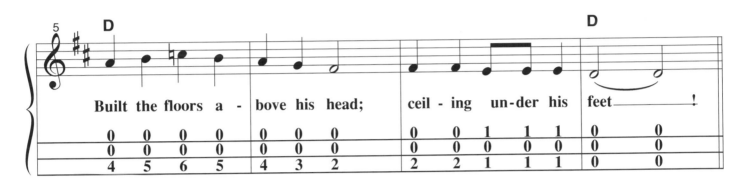

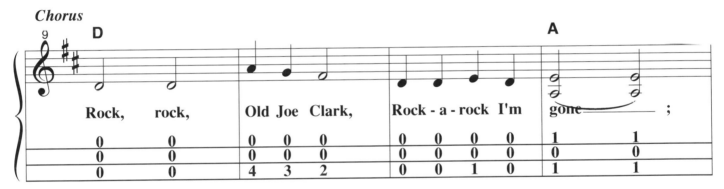

Notice that you use the 6th fret in this song. How about trying some dum-diddys at the end of each line; two dum-diddys would replace the tied half notes.

CAMPTOWN RACES

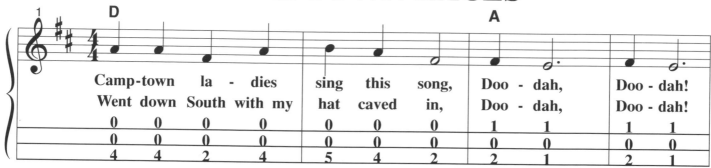

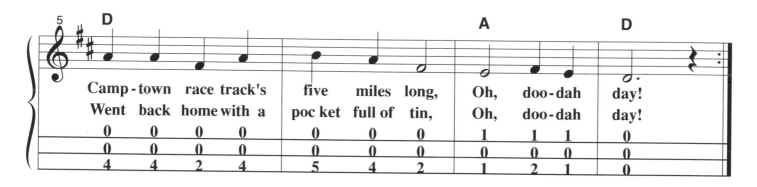

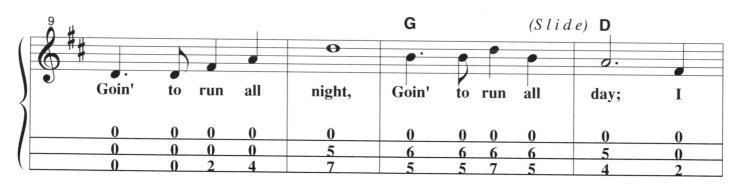

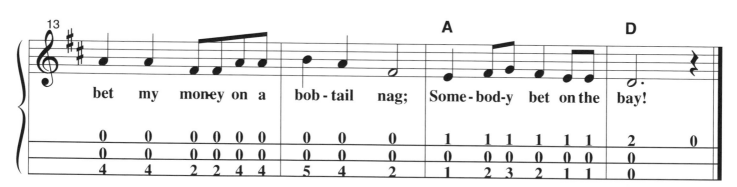

Did you notice the extra "**0**" at the very end of this song? Did you play it? It is an open plucked bass string that simply brings the song to a close. You will learn more about this technique later in this chapter.

◆ Inverting Chords . . . a DAD specialty!

In the introduction of this book, it was mentioned that the DAD tuning enabled chord inversions which enhance versatility in playing the dulcimer. A **chord inversion** is a change in the position of the pitches in a chord. For example a G chord (0-1-3) can be reversed on the fretboard to become a (3-1-0) with the 3 on the bass string instead of the melody string. You played an inverted G chord in **Simple Gifts** in Lesson Three. Try this exercise playing the original G chord for four beats followed by the inversion of the G chord for four beats.

A G chord and it's Inversion

Your 1st G chord	G chord inverted		
0 0 0 0	3 3 3 3	0 0 0 0	3 3 3 3
1 1 1 1	1 1 1 1	1 1 1 1	1 1 1 1
3 3 3 3	0 0 0 0	3 3 3 3	0 0 0 0

Notice that the only change you make is moving the 3rd fret position from the melody string to the bass string. It's the same chord; the pitches have just been reversed. Notice, also, the slight difference in the sound. With the first G chord we hear a G in the melody; in the second chord we hear a D in the melody (the G has been moved to the bass string). Can you hear the difference? Inversions are very helpful when moving up the down the fretboard with our melodies.

The rest of the songs in this chapter will utilize inverted chords, especially on the lower melody notes. See if you can identify them as you work on each song.

◆ Embellishing Our Music With Plucks!

Sometimes music tablature adds addtional notes to enhance the sound and feel of a piece of music. You've noticed this in some earlier songs. The following songs will also have some additional notes to help the music flow. They can be omitted but you will probably like what you hear when you add them. They will appear as "extra" numbers on your tablature. For example, in **Amazing Grace** there are extra notes in measures 5, 8, 9,13, 16, & 17. Can you find them? Look for embellishment notes in the rest of the songs that follow.

◆ Fingering the Frets (One last thing to think about!)

As you become more advanced with your playing, you will learn to experiment with different fingering patterns in order to reach frets, maintain a smooth melody line and keep your rhythm steady. Although I have offered fingering suggestions throughout this instruction book, remember that no two of us have the same size, shape and flexibility in our hands. What works for me may not be your best fingering pattern. Feel free to create your own fingering patterns to suit your specific needs. When working through each song be aware of awkward fingering patterns or difficult rhythm patterns. If a fingering pattern *looks* or *feels* awkward there is probably another way that will work better for you. Experiment!

◆ And Most of All . . . Have Fun!

My main goal in writing this book has been to provide a friendly beginning instruction book for the novice musician. I hope you have had *fun* with these lessons and worked at a pace that was comfortable for you. You now have the techniques and musical knowledge to continue playing and enjoying your dulcimer and trying some new music. You will probably want to continue working in the DAD tuning for awhile. When " jamming" with other dulcimers players tell them that you are playing in DAD. All the songs in this book are written in the key of D; however, this tuning also allows you to play in the keys of G and E minor quite easily.

So . . . let's take a look at a few more songs as we complete this instruction book . . . **ENJOY!**

AMAZING GRACE

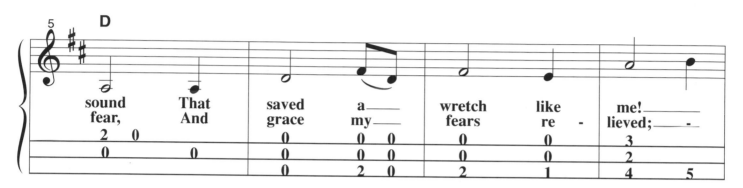

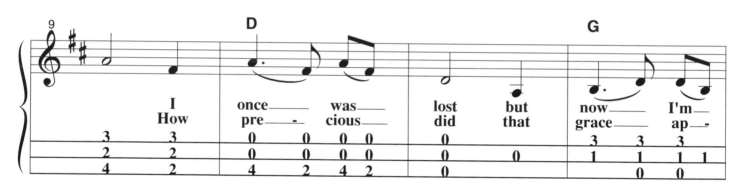

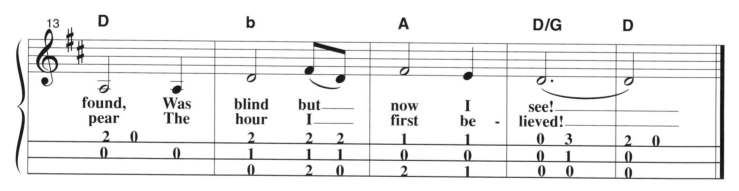

Did you notice the inverted G chords in measures 4 and 12? Embellishments were added in measures 5, 8, 9, 13, 16, & 17.

SWING LOW, SWEET CHARIOT

Chorus

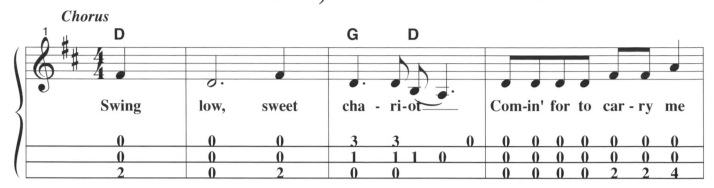

Fine   Verses 1 & 2

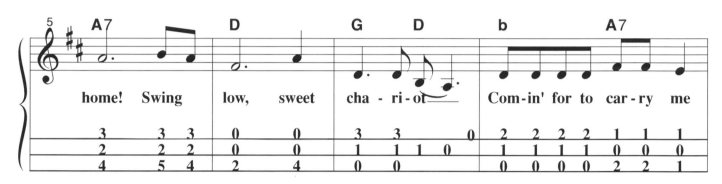

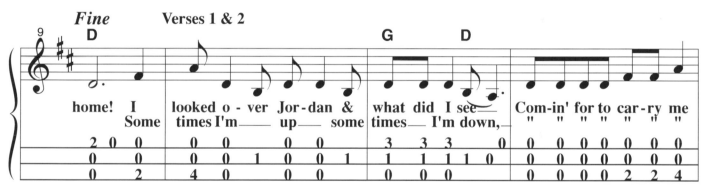

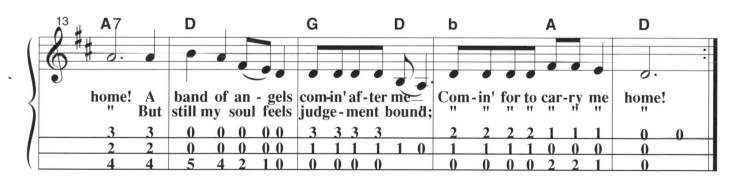

HOME ON THE RANGE

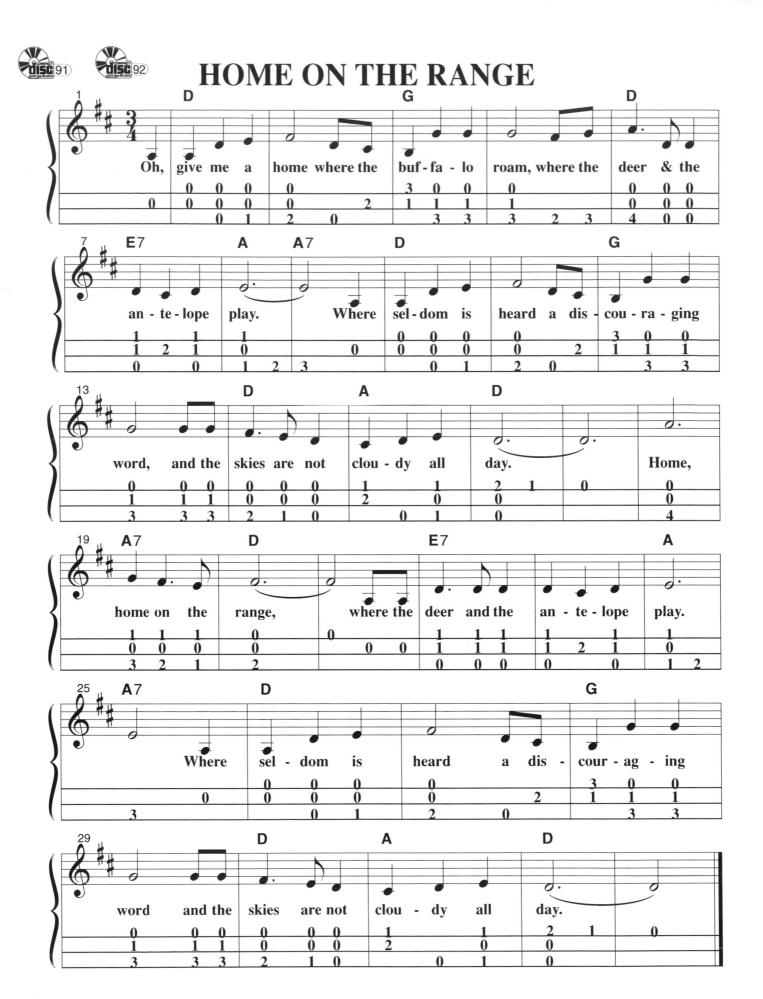

ABOUT THIS BOOK

First Lessons® Dulcimer
DAD Tuning

by Joyce Ochs

This instruction book for beginning lap dulcimer in DAD tuning is unique in two ways. First, it instructs the beginning student in the increasingly popular DAD tuning. Secondly, the author, a classroom music teacher, has carefully and systematically layered the lessons to guide the student through familiar songs while teaching skills and musical concepts. This not only enables the student to enjoy the lap dulcimer but also enhances total music understanding and participation. Includes online access to accompanying audio recording that provides instructional dialogue and demonstrations of the techniques and songs included in the book. Additional hints and exercises are presented in an inviting and encouraging conversational text.

Toll Free 1-800-8-MEL BAY (1-800-863-5229)
Fax (636) 257-5062
email@melbay.com

www.MELBAY.com

MB98388M
$14.99 USD

$14.99

ISBN 978-078-668-749-7

51499

9 780786 687497